The Sutra on the
Full Awareness of Breathing

The Sutra on the
Full Awareness of Breathing

with Commentary by Thich Nhat Hanh

Translated from the Vietnamese
by Annabel Laity

Parallax Press
Berkeley, California

Parallax Press
P.O. Box 7355
Berkeley, California 94707

Cover illustration by Vu Nguyen.
Cover design by Gay Reineck.
Composed in 10 point Bookman
on Macintosh SE by Parallax Press.

Library of Congress Cataloging in Publication Data
Tipitaka. Suttapitaka. Majjhimanikaya. Anapanasatisutta. English & Pali
The sutra on the full awareness of breathing: with commentary by
Thich Nhat Hanh / translated from the Vietnamese by Annabel Laity.
Translation of: Anapanasatisutta.
ISBN 0-938077-04-X
I. Nhât Hanh, Thich. II. Laity, Annabel. III. Title.
BQ1320.A4822E5 1988
294.3'823—dc19   88-15894

Contents

A Note on the Translation

There are several conventions employed in this translation about which it would be useful to inform the reader.

The word for a Buddhist scripture, the teachings of the Buddha, is *sutta* in Pali and *sutra* in Sanskrit. This text, the *Anapanasati Sutta*, is of Pali origin, so it would be natural to use the Pali word *sutta* throughout the text. However, due to historical circumstance, Mahayana Sanskrit scriptures have become better known in the West, so we have decided to use the word *sutra* as if it were an English word. We use the word *sutta* only when it is part of the proper name of a Pali sutta, such as *Anapanasati Sutta* or *Satipatthana Sutta*. Otherwise, we use the word *sutra* to refer even to Pali texts.

Secondly, there are no diacritical marks in this translation because of the limitations of the publisher's software. We hope to include diacritical marks for Pali and Sanskrit words in future editions.

Finally, we translate the term *sati* differently in the words *Anapanasati* and *Satipatthana*. In the former, we use "full awareness," and in the latter "mindfulness," as the *Satipatthana* is now well known as the Four Foundations of Mindfulness.

The Sutra on the
Full Awareness of Breathing

The Sutra on the Full Awareness of Breathing

Section One

This is what I have heard:

At that time the Buddha was staying in Savatthi[1] in the Eastern Park, with many well-known and accomplished disciples, including Sariputra, Maha-Moggallana, Maha-Kassapa, Maha-Kaccayana, Maha Kotthita, Maha-Kappina, Maha-Cunda, Anuruddha, Rewata, and Ananda. The senior bhikkhus[2] in the community were diligently instructing bhikkhus who were new to the practice—some instructing 10 students, some 20, some 30, and some 40; and in this way the bhikkhus new to the practice, little by little, made great progress.

That night the moon was full, and the Pavarana Ceremony[3] was held to mark the end of the rainy-season retreat. Lord Buddha, the Awakened One, was sitting in the open, and his disciples, the bhikkhus, were gathered around him. After looking over the assembly, he began speaking:

"Reverend bhikkhus, I am pleased to observe the fruit you have attained in your practice. And I know you can make even more progress. What you have not yet attained, you can attain. What you have not yet realized, you can realize perfectly. [To encourage your efforts,] I will stay here until the next full moon day."[4]

When they heard that the Lord Buddha was going to stay at Savatthi for another month, bhikkhus throughout the country began traveling there to study with him. The senior, more advanced bhikkhus, continued teaching the bhikkhus new to the practice even more ardently. Some were instructing 10 students, some 20, some 30, and some 40. With this help, the newer bhikkhus were able, little by little, to continue their progress in understanding.

When the next full moon day arrived, the Buddha, seated under the open sky, looked over the assembly of bhikkhus and began speaking:

"Reverend bhikkhus, our community is pure and good. At its heart, it is without useless and boastful talk, and therefore it deserves to receive offerings and be considered a field of merit.[5] Such a community is rare, and any pilgrim who seeks it, no matter how far he must travel, will find it worthy.

"O bhikkhus, there are bhikkhus in this assembly who have already realized the fruit of Arahathood,[6] destroyed every root of affliction,[7] laid aside every burden, and attained right understanding and emancipation. There are also bhikkhus who have already cut off the first five ropes of bondage[8] and realized the fruit of never returning to the cycle of birth and death.[9]

There are those who have thrown off the first three ropes of bondage and realized the fruit of returning once more.[10] They have cut off the roots of greed, hatred, and ignorance, and only need to return to the cycle of birth and death one more time. There are those who have thrown off the three ropes of bondage and attained the fruit of stream enterer,[11] heading steadily to the Awakened State. There are those who practice the Four Foundations of Mindfulness.[12] There are those who practice the Four Right Efforts[13] and those who practice the Four Bases of Success.[14] There are those who practice the Five Faculties,[15] those who practice the Five Powers,[16] those who practice the Seven Factors of Awakening,[17] and those who practice the Noble Eightfold Path.[18] There are those who practice Lovingkindness, those who practice Compassion, those who practice Joy, and those who practice Equanimity.[19] There are those who practice the Nine Contemplations,[20] and those who practice the Observation of Impermanence. There are also bhikkhus already practicing Full Awareness of Breathing.

Section Two

"O bhikkhus, the method of being fully aware of breathing, if developed and practiced continuously, will have great rewards and bring great advantages. It will lead to success in practicing the Four Foundations of Mindfulness. If the method of the Four Foundations of Mindfulness is developed and practiced continuously, it will lead to success in the practice of the Seven Factors of Awakening. The Seven Factors of Awakening, if developed and practiced continuously, will give rise to Understanding and Liberation of the Mind.

"What is the way to develop and practice continuously the method of Full Awareness of Breathing so that the practice will be rewarding and offer great benefit?

"It is like this, bhikkhus: the practitioner goes into the forest or to the foot of a tree, or to any deserted place, and sits stably in the lotus position, holding his body quite straight. Breathing in, he knows that he is breathing in; and breathing out, he knows that he is breathing out.

1. Breathing in a long breath, he knows, 'I am breathing in a long breath.' Breathing out a long breath, he knows, 'I am breathing out a long breath.'

2. Breathing in a short breath, he knows, 'I am breathing in a short breath.' Breathing out a short breath, he knows, 'I am breathing out a short breath.'

3. 'I am breathing in and am aware of my whole body. I am breathing out and am aware of my whole body.' This is how he practices.

4. 'I am breathing in and making my whole body calm and at peace. I am breathing out and making

my whole body calm and at peace.' This is how he practices.

5. 'I am breathing in and feeling joyful. I am breathing out and feeling joyful.'[21] This is how he practices.

6. 'I am breathing in and feeling happy. I am breathing out and feeling happy.' He practices like this.

7. 'I am breathing in and am aware of the activities of the mind in me. I am breathing out and am aware of the activities of the mind in me.' He practices like this.

8. 'I am breathing in and making the activities of the mind in me calm and at peace. I am breathing out and making the activities of the mind in me calm and at peace.' He practices like this.

9. 'I am breathing in and am aware of my mind. I am breathing out and am aware of my mind.' He practices like this.

10. 'I am breathing in and making my mind happy and at peace. I am breathing out and making my mind happy and at peace.' He practices like this.

11. 'I am breathing in and concentrating my mind. I am breathing out and concentrating my mind.' He practices like this.

12. 'I am breathing in and liberating my mind. I am breathing out and liberating my mind.' He practices like this.

13. 'I am breathing in and observing the impermanent nature of all dharmas. I am breathing out and observing the impermanent nature of all dharmas.'[22] He practices like this.

14. 'I am breathing in and observing the fading of all dharmas. I am breathing out and observing the fading of all dharmas.'[23] He practices like this.

15. 'I am breathing in and contemplating liberation. I am breathing out and contemplating liberation.'[24] He practices like this.

16. 'I am breathing in and contemplating letting go. I am breathing out and contemplating letting go.'[25] He practices like this.

The Full Awareness of Breathing, if developed and practiced continuously according to these instructions will be rewarding and of great benefit.

Section Three

"In what way does one develop and continuously practice the Full Awareness of Breathing, in order to succeed in the practice of the Four Foundations of Mindfulness?

"When the practitioner breathes in or breathes out a long or a short breath, aware of his breath or his whole body, or aware that he is making his whole body calm and at peace, he abides peacefully in the observation of the body in the body, persevering, fully awake, clearly understanding his state, gone beyond all attachment and aversion to this life. In this case, breathing in and breathing out with Full Awareness belong to the first Foundation of Mindfulness, namely the body.

"When the practitioner breathes in or out with the awareness of joy or happiness, or awareness of the activities of the mind; when the practitioner breathes in or out in order to make the activities of his mind calm and at peace, at that time he abides peacefully in the observation of the feelings in the feelings, persevering, fully awake, clearly understanding his state, gone beyond all attachment and aversion to this life. This exercise of breathing with awareness belongs to the second Foundation of Mindfulness, namely the feelings.

"When the practitioner breathes in or breathes out with the awareness of the mind, or to make the mind calm and at peace, to collect the mind in concentration, or to free and liberate the mind, at that time he abides peacefully in the observation of the mind in the mind, persevering, fully awake, clearly understanding his state, gone beyond all attachment and aversion to this life. Without full awareness of breathing, there can be no development of meditative stability and understanding.

"When the practitioner breathes in or breathes out and contemplates the essential impermanence or the essential fading of all dharmas or liberation or letting go, at that time he abides peacefully in the awareness of the objects of the mind in the objects of the mind, persevering, fully awake, clearly understanding his state, gone beyond all attachment and aversion to this life.

"The practice of Full Awareness of Breathing, if developed and practiced continuously, will lead to perfect accomplishment of the Four Foundations of Mindfulness.

Section Four

"Moreover, if they are developed and continuously practiced, the Four Foundations of Mindfulness will lead to perfect abiding in the Seven Factors of Awakening. How is this so?

"When the practitioner can maintain, without distraction, the practice of observing the body in the body, the feelings in the feelings, the mind in the mind, and the objects of mind in the objects of mind, persevering, fully awake, clearly understanding his state, gone beyond all attachment and aversion to this life, with unwavering, steadfast, imperturbable meditative stability, he will attain the first Factor of Awakening, namely Full Attention. When this factor is developed, it will come to perfection.

"When the practitioner can abide in meditative stability without being distracted and can investigate every dharma, every object of mind that arises, then the second Factor of Awakening will be born and developed in him, the factor of Investigating Dharmas. When this factor is developed, it will come to perfection.

"When the practitioner can observe and investigate every dharma in a sustained, persevering, and steadfast way, without being distracted, the third Factor of Awakening will be born and developed in him, the factor of Energy. When this factor is developed, it will come to perfection.

"When the practitioner has reached a stable, imperturbable abiding in the stream of practice, the fourth Factor of Awakening will be born and developed in him, the factor of Rapture Beyond the Everyday World.[26] When this factor is developed, it will come to perfection.

"When the practitioner can abide undistractedly in the state of rapture, he will feel his body and mind light and at peace. At this point the fifth Factor of Awakening will be born and developed, the factor of Lightness and Peacefulness. When this factor is developed, it will come to perfection.

"When both body and mind are light and at peace, the practitioner can easily enter into concentration. At that time the sixth Factor of Awakening will be born and developed in him, the factor of

Concentration. When this factor is developed, it will come to perfection.

"When the practitioner is abiding in concentration with deep calmness, he will cease discriminating and comparing.[27] At that time the seventh factor of Awakening is released, born, and developed in him, the factor of Equanimity.[28] When this factor is developed, it will come to perfection.

"This is how the Four Foundations of Mindfulness, if developed and practiced continuously, will lead to perfect abiding in the Seven Factors of Awakening.

Section Five

"How will the Seven Factors of Awakening, if developed and practiced continuously, lead to the perfect accomplishment of true understanding and complete liberation?

"If the practitioner follows the path of the Seven Factors of Awakening, living in quiet seclusion, observing and contemplating the fading of all dharmas, he will develop the capacity of letting go. This will be a result of following the path of the Seven Factors of Awakening and will lead to the perfect accomplishment of true understanding and complete liberation."

Section Six

This is what the Lord, the Awakened One, said; and everyone in the assembly felt gratitude and delight at having heard his teachings.

Commentary on the Sutra
by Thich Nhat Hanh

Chapter One
A Brief History

The Sutra on the Full Awareness of Breathing presented here is a translation of the *Anapanasati Sutta.*[29] In the Chinese Tripitaka there is a *Greater Anapanasati Sutta (Da An Ban Shou Yi Jing)*,[30] but no *Simple Anapanasati Sutta (An Ban Shou Yi Jing)*. Usually in the Canon, if a scripture is entitled "Greater," it was expanded from the original during the process of oral transmission or as it was being copied. Therefore, a scripture which does not have the word *Greater* in the title is probably closer to the original words of the Buddha.

The *Da An Ban Shou Yi Jing*[31] gives the name of An Shi Gao, a Parthian by birth who went to China in the later Han period, as the translator, and has a preface written by Master Tang Hôi. This text seems to be different from the *Anapanasati*, and is probably a commentary on it and not just an expansion or embellishment of it. At the end of the text, the engraver of the wood block says, "Judging from the style of the sutra, it seems the copyist is at fault: the original text and the commentary are so intertwined that it is no longer possible to distinguish between them."

We think that the original translation of the Sanskrit (or Prakrit) text into Chinese has been lost. In the Chinese Tripitaka is the commentary which was originally printed below the text of the sutra. It does not begin with the words which usually begin a sutra, "This is what I have heard." According to Tang Hôi's preface, the person responsible for the annotation and commentary was Chen Hui, and Tang Hôi himself only assisted in the work of correcting, altering, and editing.

Chen Hui was a disciple of Master An Shi Gao, who traveled from Loyang to Giao Chi (present-day Vietnam) with two fellow disciples, Gan Lin and Pi Ye. They may have brought the original translation of the *Anapanasati Sutta* with them. The commentary and preface were written by Tang Hôi in Vietnam before the year 229 C.E.

Tang Hôi was born in Vietnam. His mother and father were traders from Sogdia who passed through Vietnam and settled there. Tang Hôi became a monk and studied Sanskrit and Chinese there. Before traveling to the kingdom of Wu in southern China in the year 255 to spread the Dharma, he had already taught the Dharma in Vietnam and composed and translated many works into Chinese. He died in the kingdom of Wu in the year 280.

In the Chinese Tripitaka, there are a number of other Sutras on the Full Awareness of Breathing: *Zeng Yi A Han (Ekottaragama)*, the chapter on "Awareness of Breathing," books 7 and 8;[32] and the sutra *Xiu Hang Dao Di*, book 5, chapter 23, on "Breath Counting."[33] In both these writings, we rediscover the simple and original spirit of the *Anapanasati* from the Pali Canon.

The sutra presented here in English has been translated from the original *Anapanasati Sutta* in the Pali Tripitaka. In many countries of the Mahayana tradition, the *Anapanasati Sutta (Full Awareness of Breathing)* and the *Satipatthana Sutta (Four Foundations of Mindfulness)* are not available for study. These two texts are fundamental to the practice of meditation, and the author of this commentary feels that it is important to re-establish them in all places of study and meditation.

The *Full Awareness of Breathing* and the *Four Foundations of Mindfulness* are still regarded as the most important texts for the Southern Schools of Buddhism. Many monks learn these sutras by heart. The author hopes that these two sutras will again be put into wide circulation in the Northern Schools of Buddhism. Even though the spirit of these sutras is present and observable in the Mahayana meditation sutras, we would do well to become familiar with these sutras themselves. This is the literature fundamental to meditation which was studied and practiced at the time of the Buddha. If we understand the essence of these two sutras, we will have a deeper vision and more comprehensive grasp of the sutras classified as Mahayana, just as after we see the roots and the trunk of a tree, we can appreciate its leaves and branches.

From these two sutras, we can see that practitioners of meditation at the time of the Buddha had not yet come into contact with the Four Meditative States[34] and the Four Formless Concentrations.[35] The Four Meditative States are mental states in which the practitioner abandons the desire realm and enters the realm of form, and although his or her mind remains perfectly awake, the five sense perceptions no longer arise. There are four successive states (also called Four Absorptions), which are followed by the Four Formless Concentrations. These are states of meditation in which the practitioner has already abandoned the form realm and entered the formless realm: (1) The Realm of Limitless Space, (2) The Realm of Limitless Consciousness, (3) The Realm of No Materiality, and (4) The Realm Where the Concepts "Perceiving" and "Not Perceiving" No Longer Apply. There are occasional references in other sutras of the Southern Schools as well as in those of the Northern Schools to the Four Meditative States and the Four Formless Concentrations. It is only in these two basic sutras (*Full Awareness of Breathing* and *Four Foundations of Mindfulness*) that we see no such references. Thus we can infer that the Four Meditative States and the Four Formless Concentrations were instituted after the death of the Buddha, probably due to the influence of Vedic and other Yogic meditation schools outside of Buddhism.

Therefore we may conclude that according to the *Anapanasati* and *Satipatthana Suttas*, the realization of the Four Meditative States and the Four Formless Concentrations is dispensable. Future generations of scholars should distinguish as much as possible between the essential, fundamental meditation practices of Buddhism (whether Northern or Southern), and elements which were incorporated later from other traditions.

Analyzing their content, we can see that the *Anapanasati* and *Satipatthana Suttas* are perfectly compatible with one another. Throughout 2,500 years of Buddhist history, all generations of Buddha's disciples have respected these works and have not embellished them (as they did so many other scriptures). Although the *Anapanasati Sutta* was in circulation in Vietnam as early as the second century, from the time Vietnamese Buddhism came under the influence of the Northern Schools, this sutra ceased to be regarded as most essential. It is time for us to restore this sutra to its proper place in the tradition of meditation practice.

Chapter Two
Summary of the Content

The sixteen different methods of inhaling and exhaling, in combination with the Four Foundations of Mindfulness, are the essence of the *Full Awareness of Breathing Sutra*. Breathing is a means of awakening and maintaining full attention in order to look carefully, long and deeply, see the nature of all things, and arrive at liberation.

Everything that exists can be placed into one of the Four Foundations of Mindfulness—namely the body, the feelings, the mind, and the objects of the mind. "All dharmas" is another way of saying "the objects of the mind." Although all dharmas are divided into four, in reality they are one, because all Four Foundations of Mindfulness are objects of the mind.

The sixteen methods of breathing in and breathing out can be divided into four groups of four methods each. The first group uses the body as the object of Full Awareness; the second uses the feelings; the third, the mind; and the fourth, the objects of mind.

After explaining the sixteen methods of Fully Aware Breathing, the Buddha speaks about the Four Foundations of Mindfulness and the Seven Factors of Awakening. He then reminds us that if the methods of Fully Aware Breathing are practiced continuously, they will lead to the successful accomplishment of the Seven Factors of Awakening. The Buddha speaks in greater detail about the Four Foundations of Mindfulness in the *Satipatthana Sutta*. The Seven Factors of Awakening are also discussed again in the *Anapanasati Sutta* and in other sutras. The main point of this sutra is the practice of Full Awareness of Breathing combined with the practice of the Four Foundations of Mindfulness.

Chapter Three
Analysis of the Sutra's Content

The *Sutra on the Full Awareness of Breathing* can be divided into six sections:

Section One - The Scene

The first part of the sutra describes the circumstances under which the Buddha delivered this lecture. We are told about the community of his disciples during the time he was staying at the Eastern Park, a very large park with many trees located right in the town of Savatthi. The number of monks staying with the Buddha at that time may have been more than 400. The senior monks each taught 10, 20, 30 or 40 newer monks.

Every morning after sitting in meditation, the monks would go into the town together, bowls in hand, to beg for food. Before mid-day, when the sun was directly overhead, they returned to their retreat center to eat. From time to time, they would all be invited to eat at the king's palace or at the home of a wealthy patron, someone whose home was large enough to accommodate so many monks. Poorer households would wait for the bhikkhus to walk by, so they too could make offerings. There were also some people who would bring food to the retreat center to offer to the community.

The Buddha and his disciples ate only one meal a day, before noon. There was no cooking or baking in the retreat center itself. The monks had no responsibility for performing funerals or praying for sick or deceased laypersons, as is the case today in many countries. Instead they offered a brief lecture to their sponsors either before or after eating the meal offered by them. They spoke clearly and powerfully, because they were living an integrated life, putting their study into practice.

While the sun was still up, the Buddha would teach his disciples under the shade of a grove of trees. Sometimes, if the moon was bright, he would also give a lecture in the evening, as was the case with this sutra. The Buddha had previously explained aspects of the practice of the Full Awareness of Breathing a number of times (we know that there were many disciples already practicing it), but the evening he delivered this sutra was probably the first time he taught the entire method systematically and completely. He probably chose this occasion because there were many bhikkhus from all around the country present, including a number of new disciples. Many were able to be there because they had completed their rainy-season retreats one month earlier than the monks staying at the Eastern Park retreat center. That year the retreat of the Buddha and his disciples in the Eastern Park was extended an additional month, to four months, so that there could be a chance for disciples from the entire country to be in one place together. There may have been as many as 1,000 bhikkhus present the evening the Lord Buddha delivered the Sutra on the Full Awareness of Breathing.

Section Two - The Sixteen Methods

The second section is the heart of the sutra. This section elaborates the sixteen methods of Fully Aware Breathing in connection with the Four Foundations of Mindfulness.

1. The Four Preliminary Methods

In Methods One and Two, the object of awareness is the breath itself. The mind of the one who is breathing is the subject, and his or her breathing is the object. These breaths may be short, long, heavy, or light. We see that our breathing effects our mind, and our mind effects our breathing. The mind and the breath become one. We also see that breathing is an aspect of the body and that awareness of breathing is also awareness of the body.

In the third method, the breath is connected with the whole body, not just a part of it. Awareness of the breathing is, at the same time, awareness of the entire body. The mind, the breath, and the whole body are one.

In the fourth breathing method, the body's functions begin calming down. The calming of the breath is accompanied by the calming of the body and the mind. The mind, the breathing, and the body are each calmed down equally.

In just four breathing exercises, we can realize oneness of body and mind. Breathing is an excellent tool for establishing calmness and even-mindedness.

2. The Second Four Methods

The fifth method brings us into contact with our feelings. There are three kinds of feelings: pleasant, unpleasant, and neutral (neither pleasant nor unpleasant). As a result of conscious breathing and calming the body (Skt: kaya-samskara), joy arises. This pleasant feeling arises naturally from the fourth method.

In the sixth method, joy is transformed into peace and happiness, and we are fully aware of it. The seventh and eighth methods bring our attention to all feelings which arise, whether produced by the body or the mind (citta-samskara). The mind's functions include feelings and perceptions. When we are aware of every bodily and every mental action, we are aware of every feeling.

The eighth method calms the body and mind and renders them peaceful. At this point, we can unify body, mind, feelings, and breath, perfectly and completely.

3. The Next Four Methods

In the ninth through twelfth methods, the mind is the object. "Mind" (citta) consists of all the functions of the mind, including feelings, perceptions, and all psychological states. Buddhist psychology lists 51 mental functions (citta-samskara). However, "mind" is also consciousness, discrimination, and reflection; and awareness during the ninth breathing method includes all of these, whatever is arising in the mind in the present moment.

The tenth method makes our mind joyful, because it is easier for the mind to become concentrated when it is in a peaceful, happy state than when it is filled with sorrow or anxiety. We are aware that we have the opportunity to practice meditation and that there is no moment as important as the present one. Calmly abiding in the present moment, immense joy arises.

Using the mind to observe the mind, the eleventh method brings us to deep concentration. Mind is the breath. Mind is the oneness of the subject which observes and illumines and the object which is observed and illumined. Mind is peace and happiness. Mind is the field of illumination and the strength of concentration.

The twelfth method can release the mind to freedom, if it is still bound. Mind is bound either because of the past or the future, or because of other latent desires or anger. With clear observation, we can locate the knots which hold us, making it impossible for the mind to be free and at peace. Loosening these knots, we can untie the ropes which bind our mind. Full Awareness of Breathing breathes into the mind the light of observation which can illumine and set the mind free.

4. The Four Final Methods

Mind cannot be separated from its object. Mind is consciousness, feeling, attachment, aversion, and so on. Consciousness must always be conscious of something. Feeling is always feeling something. Loving and hating are always loving and hating something. This "something" is the object of the mind. Mind cannot arise if there is no object. Mind does not exist if the object of mind does not exist. The mind is, at one and the same time, the subject of consciousness and the object of consciousness. All physiological phenomena, such as the breath, the nervous system, and the sense organs; all psychological phenomena, such as feelings, thought, and consciousness; and all physical phenomena, such as the earth, water, grass, trees, mountains, and rivers, are objects of mind; and therefore all are mind. All of them can be called "dharmas."

The thirteenth breathing method sheds light on the ever-changing, impermanent nature of all that exists—the psychological, the physiological, and the physical. Breathing itself is also impermanent. The fact of impermanence is very important, because it opens the way for us to see the inter-related, inter-conditioned nature as well as the self-less nature (nothing has a separate, independent self) of all that exists.

The fourteenth method allows us to see that every dharma is already in the process of dis-integrating (fading) so that we are no longer possessed by the idea of holding onto any dharma as a separate entity, even the physiological and psychological elements in ourselves.

The fifteenth allows us to arrive at the awareness of a great joy, the joy of emancipation, by freeing us from the intention to catch, hold, or grasp any dharma.

The sixteenth method illuminates for us what it is to let go of ourselves, to give up all the burdens of our ignorance and our grasping. To be able to let go is already to have arrived at liberation.

These sixteen methods can be studied and practiced intelligently. Although the four preliminary methods help our concentration very much, and every time we practice it is helpful to do these, it is not always necessary to practice the sixteen methods in this order. For example, you might like to practice only the fourteenth method for several days or months.

Although these methods are presented very simply, their effectiveness is immeasurable. Depending on your experience, you can enter them deeply or superficially. The Lord Buddha did not intend to generate new theories, to confuse the minds of those new to the practice, so he used simple terms, like impermanence, fading away, emancipation, and letting go. In fact, the term impermanence also includes the concepts of no-self, emptiness, interconnectedness, signlessness (*alaksana*) and aimlessness (*apranihita*). That is why, in progressing, it is so important to observe that which illumines and leads to emancipation.

Section Three - 4 Foundations of Mindfulness

The third part of the sutra is concerned with the Four Foundations of Mindfulness. These are referred to in the second section, although not by name. In this sutra, the Four Foundations are only briefly referred to and expounded. We must read the *Satipatthana Sutta* to know the subject in more detail.[36] The Four Foundations are the body, the feelings, the mind, and all dharmas (objects of mind). In this sutra, the work of being fully aware of the Four Foundations is through conscious breathing.

I wish to say something about the expressions "observing the body in the body," "observing the feelings in the feelings," "observing the mind in the mind," and "observing the objects of mind in the objects of mind." The key to "observation meditation" is that the subject of the observation and the object of the observation not be regarded as two separate things. A scientist might try to separate him or herself from the object he or she is observing and measuring, but students of meditation have to remove the boundary between subject and object. When we observe something, we *are* that thing. Nonduality is the key word. "Observing the body in the body" means that in the process of observing, we do not stand outside our own body like an independent observer, but we identify with the object being observed. This is the only path that can lead us to the penetration and direct experience of reality. In "observation meditation," the body and mind are one entity, and the subject and object of meditation are one entity also. In "observation meditation," there is no sword of discrimination which slices reality into parts. The meditator is a fully engaged participant, not a separate observer.

"Observation meditation" is a lucid awareness of what is going on in the Four Foundations: body, feelings, mind, and all dharmas, "persevering, fully awake, clearly understanding his state, gone beyond all attachment and aversion to this life." "Life" means all that exists. Stubbornly clinging to all that exists or resisting and rejecting it all both lack the lucidity of an awakened mind. In order to succeed in the work of observation, we must go beyond both attachment and aversion.

Section Four - 7 Factors of Awakening

In the fourth section of the sutra, the Buddha discusses the arising, growth, and attainment of the Seven Factors of Awakening, through abiding in them in conjunction with conscious breathing.

(1) Full Attention is the main Factor of Awakening. Full Attention is awareness, being fully awake. If Full Attention is developed and maintained, the practice of observation to shed light on and see clearly all that exists will meet with success. (2) The work of observation to shed light on and see clearly all that exists is Investigation of Dharmas. (3) Energy is perseverance and diligence. (4-5) Rapture, Lightness, and Peacefulness are joyful feelings nourished by energy. (6) Concentration gives rise to understanding. When we have understanding, we can go beyond all comparing, measuring, discriminating, and reacting with attach-

ment and aversion. (7) Going beyond is Equanimity. Those who arrive at Equanimity will have the bud of a half-smile, which proves compassion as well as understanding.

Section Five - Emancipation

In the fifth section, which is very short, the Buddha reminds us that the Seven Factors of Awakening, if practiced diligently, lead to true understanding and emancipation.

Section Six - Conclusion

The sixth section is the concluding sentence of the sutra. This sentence is used at the end of every sutra.

Chapter Four
A Point of View on the Practice

Neither the *Sutra on the Full Awareness of Breathing* nor the *Sutra on the Four Foundations of Mindfulness* mentions the method of counting the breath. There is also no mention of the Six Wonderful Dharma Doors: counting, following, stopping, observing, returning, and calming. Nor is there any reference to the *kasina* (sign) meditation, the Four Meditative States, and the Four Formless Concentrations. These teachings were probably developed a little later in order to serve many levels of students. We need not criticize them for being later teachings, certainly not before we have practiced them and seen for ourselves if they work well.[37]

Counting is an excellent method for beginners. Breathing in, count "one." Breathing out, count "one." Breathing in, count "two." Breathing out, count "two." Continue up to ten and then start again. If at any time you forget where you are, begin again with "one." The method of counting helps us refrain from dwelling on troublesome thoughts; instead we concentrate on our breathing and the number. When we have developed some control over our thinking, counting may become burdensome, and we can abandon it and just follow the breath itself. This is called "Following."

Well-known commentaries, such as the *Pati-sambhida Magga* (*Path of No Hesitation*) and the *Visuddhi Magga* (*Path of Purification*), teach that while we breathe, we should be aware of our nostrils, the place where air enters and leaves the body. Just as when we cut a log we keep our eyes on the place where the saw touches the log (rather than looking at the teeth of the saw), we pay attention to the nostrils, and not to the air as it enters the body. Many commentators note that if you follow the breath entering the body, then the object of your attention is not a single object, and concentration will be difficult. For this reason, they say that "the whole body" in the third method means the whole body of breath and not the whole body of the practitioner. If we study the sutra, we can see that their explanation is not correct. In the third breathing method, the object of attention is not just the breath. It *is* the whole body of the practitioner, in the same way that the object of the seventh method is all feelings and the object of the ninth method is the whole mind.

In the fourth method ("I am breathing in and making my whole body calm and at peace"), the expression "whole body" cannot mean just the whole body of breath either. All four preliminary methods take the physical body as the object, since the body is the first of the Four Foundations of Mindfulness. Even if in the first two methods the object is just the breathing, that includes the body, since the breath is a part of our physical organism. In the third and fourth methods, the entire physical body is the object.

The reason the commentaries, *Patisambhida Magga* (*Path of No Hesitation*), by Mahanama, *Vimutti Magga* (*Path of Liberation*), by Upatissa, and the *Visuddhi Magga* (*Path of Purification*), by Buddhaghosa, recommend that practitioners focus on the tip of the nose rather than following the breath as it enters the body, is that they say if the "psychological factors" follow the breath into the body, the practitioner will be dispersed and unable to enter into the Four Meditations. The *Vimutti Magga* was written at the end of the fourth century C.E., the *Patisambhida Magga* at the beginning of the fifth, and the *Visuddhi Magga* shortly after that. All three of these emphasize "stopping" (*samatha*) as the prerequisite for "observing" (*vipasyana*). Here, stopping means the Four Meditations and the Four Formless Concentrations. If the practitioner focuses his mind at the tip of his nose and is aware of the first moment of contact of air at its place of entry into the body (just as the carpenter looks only at the place of contact of the saw's teeth as they enter and leave the wood), gradually his rough, uneven breathing will become gentle and subtle, and then all discrimination will disappear. At this point, the sign (*kasina*) will appear, like a ball of cotton, giving him a feeling of freshness, lightness, and ease, like a cool breeze. If he follows this sign, he will enter concentration, the first of the Four Meditations. The First Meditation is followed by the second, third, and fourth Meditative States. In each state of meditative concentration, the five sense organs are inactive, while the practitioner's mind is lucid and awake. After the Four Meditations come the Four

Formless Concentrations: the realm of limitless space, the realm of limitless consciousness, the realm of no materiality, and the realm where the concepts "perceiving" and "not perceiving" no longer apply.

We must examine the extent to which Buddhist meditation practice was influenced by the Yoga-Upanishadic systems. Before realizing the Way, Shakyamuni Buddha studied with many Brahman yogis, from whom he learned the Four Meditations and the Four Formless Concentrations. After experiencing these, he said that concentrations like "the realm of no materiality" and "the realm where perceiving and not perceiving do not apply," taught by the masters Arada Kalama and Udraka Ramaputra, cannot lead to ultimate emancipation. As we have seen, he did not mention the Four Meditations or the Four Formless Concentrations in the *Anapanasati* or the *Satipatthana*, the two fundamental sutras on meditation. Therefore we must conclude that the practices of the Four Meditations and the Four Formless Concentrations are not a necessity for arriving at the fruit of practice, the Awakened Mind. The methods of mindfulness taught by the Buddha in the *Sutra on the Four Foundations of Mindfulness* can be seen as the incomparable path leading to emancipation. There are meditation students who have practiced for many years and who, having failed to attain the Four Meditations, think they do not have the capacity to realize Awakening. There are others who stray into unhealthy meditation practices and lose all peace of mind, just because they want so much to enter the Four Meditations. Only by practicing correctly, according to the teachings of the Buddha in the *Anapanasati* and *Satipatthana Suttas* can we be sure we will not stray into practices we may later regret.

In Vietnam, the home country of the author, at the beginning of the third century C.E., the meditation master Tang Hôi, when writing the preface to the *Anapanasati* in Chinese, referred to the Four Meditations, but the Four Meditations of Tang Hôi were combined with observation—observing the body, observing sky and earth, observing prosperity and decline, coming and going, and so forth. Tang Hôi also spoke of the Six Wonderful Dharma Doors (counting the breath, following the breath, concentrating the mind, observing to throw light on all that exists, returning to the source of mind, and going beyond the concepts of subject and object). Moreover Tang Hôi referred to the method of concentrating the mind at the tip of the nose. The *Xiu Hang Dao Di Sutta*, in the chapter called "Enumerating,"[38] also refers to the Four Meditations, the method of counting the breath, the Six Wonderful Dharma Doors, and the method of concentrating the mind at the tip of the nose. The *Zeng Yi A Han (Ekottaragama) Sutta*[39] in the chapter on breathing, also refers to the Four Meditations and to the method of concentrating the mind at the tip of the nose, but it does not refer to counting the breath or the Six Wonderful Dharma Doors.

We should remember that the sutras were memorized and transmitted orally for hundreds of years before they were written down. Therefore, many sutras must have been at least somewhat altered according to a variety of influences and circumstances during those centuries. The *Anapanasati* and *Satipatthana Suttas* can be seen as two precious accounts of early Buddhist meditation practice since they were handed down by the monks in an especially careful way. It seems to be the case that mistakes and outside additions were very few in the case of these two sutras.

In the history of Buddhism, there are some classical sutras which were affected during their transmission by outside influences forever afterwards, in the Southern schools as in the Northern schools, but especially in the Northern schools. Studying Mahayana sutras reminds us to look again and discover the depth of the fundamental "source" sutras. The seeds of all important ideas of the Mahayana are already contained in these "source" sutras. If we go back to the "source," we develop a more clear and unshakable view of the Mahayana sutras. If we merely sit on the two giant wings of the Mahayana bird, we may fly far away and lose all contact with the source from which the bird arose.

Although the *Anapanasati* and *Satipatthana Suttas* do not refer to the Four Meditations and the Four Formless Concentrations, we should not conclude that they do not stress the necessity of concentration, the importance of the power and flexibility of concentration. Meditation has two aspects: stopping (*samatha*) in order to look (*vipasyana*). Stopping is concentration and looking is understanding. The Full Awareness of the breath, or of any other object such as the body, the feelings, the consciousness, the objects of consciousness, and so on, are all aiming at the goal of concentrating the mind on an object so that it is possible to see the object in all its depth. Concentrating mind is stopping it from running from one object to another in order for it to stay with just one object. We stay with one object in order to observe it and to look deeply into it. In this way, stopping and observing become one.

Thanks to our ability to stop, we are able to observe. The more deeply we observe, the greater our mental concentration becomes. Stopping and collecting our mind, we naturally become able to see. In observing, the mind becomes increasingly still. We can say that if there is no stopping, there is no observing, and if there is no observing, there is no stopping. Although the *Anapanasati* and *Satipatthana Suttas* do not refer to the Four Meditations and the Four Formless Concentrations, the essential teaching of these two sutras is that we concentrate (stop) the mind in order to be able to see. We do not need to search for anything more. We only need to practice the simple methods proposed by the Buddha in these two sutras.

Chapter Five
Methods of Practice

The practices of stopping and observing are to arrive at liberation, the freedom from being bound. To what are we bound? First of all, there is falling back into forgetfulness, losing our mindfulness. We live as if we are in a dream. We are dragged back into the past and pulled forward into the future. We are bound by our sorrows, by holding onto anger, by feelings of unease and fear. Here "liberation" means going beyond and leaving these conditions behind in order to live fully awake, joyfully and freshly, at ease and in peace. To live in this way means that life is worth living. Living like this, we are a source of joy to our family and to those who live with us and around us. Buddhism often refers to "emancipation," i.e. going beyond and leaving birth and death behind. We feel threatened by death. How much unease and fear has been brought about by the fear of death! Meditation allows us to be free from these bonds of unease and fear.

Following are some methods for putting the *Anapanasati Sutta* into practice. They are offered in a simple way, in accord with the spirit of the sutra. Please use whatever methods suit you in your present situation, and practice them first. Although the 16 methods of practicing full awareness of the breath are intimately connected to one another, the order in which they are given in the sutra is not necessarily a progression from easy to difficult. Every method is as wonderful as every other, as easy and as difficult as every other one. We can, however, say that the preliminary instructions place greater importance on "stopping," and the later ones place more importance on "observing," although, of course, stopping and observing cannot exist separately from one another. If there is stopping, observing is already present, more or less; and if there is observing, there is a natural stopping.

The subjects for full awareness suggested below can be divided into seven categories:

1. Following the breath in daily life—eliminating forgetfulness and unnecessary thinking (Methods 1-2)

2. Awareness of the body (Method 3)

3. Realizing the unity of body and mind (Method 4)

4. Nourishing ourselves with the joy of meditation (Methods 5-6)

5. Observing in order to shine light on the feelings (Methods 7-8)

6. Controlling and liberating the mind (Methods 9-12)

7. Observing in order to shed light on the true nature of all dharmas (Methods 13-16)

Laypersons as well as monks must know how to practice both the first subject (following the breath in daily life) and the fourth (nourishing ourselves with the joy of meditation). Every time we practice sitting meditation, we should begin with these two subjects. Only after that should we go into the other subjects. Every time we notice our state of mind becoming agitated, dispersed, ill-at-ease, we should practice the fifth subject (observing in order to shine light on our feelings). The seventh subject is the door which opens onto liberation from birth and death, and all those of great understanding have to pass through this door. This subject is the greatest gift the Buddha has given us. The first six subjects all involve stopping as well as observing, but the seventh emphasizes observation. Only after we have the capacity to concentrate our mind with great stability, great concentration, should we embark on this subject.

The First Subject of Full Awareness:
Following the breath in daily life—eliminating forget-fulness and unnecessary thinking (Methods 1-2)

Most of the readers of this book do not live in forests under trees, or in monasteries. In our daily lives, we drive cars and wait for buses, work in factories and offices, talk on the telephone, clean our houses, cook meals, wash clothes, and so on. Therefore, it is most important that we learn to practice Full Awareness of Breathing during our daily lives. Usually, when we perform these tasks, our thoughts wander, and our joys, sorrows, anger, and unease follow close behind. Although we are alive, we are not able to bring our minds into the present moment, and we live in forgetfulness.

We can begin by becoming aware of our breath, by following our breathing. Breathing in and breathing out, we know we are breathing in and out, and we can smile to affirm that we are ourselves, that we are in control of ourselves. Through awareness of breathing, we can be awake in and to the present moment. By being attentive, we have already established "stopping," i.e. concentration of mind. Breathing with full awareness helps our mind stop wandering in confused, never-ending thoughts.

Most of our daily activities can be accomplished while following our breath according to the instructions in the sutra. When our work demands special attentiveness in order to avoid confusion or an accident, we can unite Full Awareness of Breathing with the task itself. For example, when we are carrying a pot of boiling water or doing electrical repairs, we can be aware of every movement of our hands, and we can nourish this awareness by means of our breath: "I am breathing out, and I am aware my hands are carrying a pot of boiling water," or "I am breathing in and I am aware that my right hand is holding an electrical wire," or even "I am breathing in and I am aware that I am passing another car. I am breathing out and I know that the situation is under control." We can practice like this.

In fact, it is not enough to combine awareness of breathing only with tasks which require so much attention. We must also combine Full Awareness of our Breathing with all the movements of our body: "I am breathing in and I am sitting down." "I am breathing in and wiping the table." "I am breathing in and smiling at myself." "I am breathing in and lighting the stove." Stopping the random progres-

sion of thoughts and living in forgetfulness is a giant step forward in meditation practice. We can realize this step by following our breath and
combining it with awareness of our daily activities.

There are people who have no peace or joy and
even go insane simply because they cannot stop
unnecessary thinking. They are forced to take
sedatives to lull themselves to sleep, just to give
their thoughts a rest. But even in their dreams,
they continue to feel fears, anxieties, and unease.
Thinking too much can cause headaches, and your
spirit will suffer.

By following your breath and combining the
Full Awareness of Breathing with your daily activities, you can cut across the stream of disturbing
thoughts and light the lamp of awakening. Full
awareness of an out-breath and an in-breath is
something wonderful that anyone can practice.
Even if you live in a monastery or a meditation
center, you can practice in this way. Combining
full awareness of breathing with full awareness of
the movements of the body during daily activities—walking, standing, lying, sitting, working—is
a basic Dharma practice to cultivate concentration
and to live in an awakened state. During the first
few minutes of sitting meditation, you can use this
method to harmonize your breathing, and if it
seems necessary, you can continue following your
breath with full awareness throughout the entire
period.

The Second Subject of Full Awareness:
Awareness of the Body (Method 3)

During the practice of meditation, body and mind become one. In the sitting, lying, standing, or walking position, we can practice awareness of the body, beginning by taking the different parts of our body one by one, and then taking the organism as a whole. We can start with our hair, and then go down to the tips of our toes. For example, when in the position of sitting meditation, after regulating your breathing, you begin by breathing out and you observe, "I am breathing out and am aware of the hair on my head." "I am breathing in and am aware of the contents of my skull." You can continue like this until you reach the tips of your toes. In the process of the practice, feelings and considerations may arise. For example, I am passing my heart and suddenly I notice anxiety rising up in me with regard to a close friend's heart condition. I do not push this feeling away, I am cognizant of it: "I am breathing in and am aware that I am anxious about my friend's heart condition." Then you continue your journey of observation of your body under the supervision of the Full Awareness of Breathing. Here is another example: When I am passing through the digestive organs, I see millions of minute living beings which are living along with me in my intestines. I do not push this perception away, I am simply cognizant of it: "I am breathing in and am aware of the minute organisms, living along with me and in me." If you see that your awareness of your symbiosis with these organisms is a rich subject for meditation, you can recognize it as such and make an appointment with yourself to return to this subject later, and then continue with your journey of observation through the rest of your body.

You know that we give very little attention to the organs of our body. We are conscious of them only when they cause us pain and when we are starting to be ill. You can pass half your life seeking riches and fame without ever holding your little toe between your fingers in awakened awareness. Your little toe is very important, you know. It has been very kind to you for many years. If one day in the future there is a sign of cancer in it, what will you do?

Perhaps you think that to be aware of the body is not very important. But that is not true. Any physiological, psychological, or physical phenomenon can be a door which leads you to truth. You can meditate on your toe and reach the goal of realization. The secret of this practice is to concentrate the mind in order to observe each organ of the body in full awareness. If you practice in this way, one day (perhaps tomorrow or even this afternoon) you may see deep and wonderful things which can change your view and way of life. The hair on your head seems very ordinary, but you should know that your hair is an ambassador of truth. Please receive the credentials of this hair. Observe them well and discover every message that each hair bears in itself. Are your eyes common physiological phenomena? They are the windows which open onto the miracle of reality. Do not neglect anything. Look deeply, and you will see. That is the practice of meditation.

The Third Subject of Full Awareness:
Realizing the Unity of Body and Mind (Method 4)

During another period of meditation, observe your whole body without discriminating between different parts: "I am breathing in and am aware of my whole body." (Method 3). At this point, let your breathing, your body, and your observing mind all become one. Breathing and body are one. Breathing and mind are one. Mind and body are one. At the time of observation, mind is not an entity which exists independently, outside of your breathing and your body. The boundary between the subject of observation and the object of observation no longer exists. We observe "the body in the body." The mind does not stand outside of the object in order to observe it. The mind is one with the object it observes. This is the first principle—"subject and object are empty (subject and object are not two)"—which has been developed extensively in the Mahayana tradition.

Practicing this way for 10 or 20 minutes, the flow of your breathing and your body become very calm, and your mind becomes much more at rest. When you first begin these practices, it seems quite rough, like coarsely milled wheat, like riding a horse for the first time, or like the sound of a church bell after its first jarring ring. But the flour becomes finer and finer, the horse rides more and more smoothly, and the sound of the bell becomes more and more beautiful. The fourth breathing method accompanies you on this path: "I am breathing in and making my whole body calm and at peace." It is like drinking a cool glass of lemonade on a hot day and feeling your body become cool inside. When you breathe in, the air enters your body and calms all the cells of your body. At the same time, each "cell" of your breathing becomes more peaceful and each "cell" of your mind also becomes more peaceful. The three are one and each one is all three. This is the key to meditation. If the horse trots peacefully, the rider rides peacefully. And the more relaxed the rider feels, the more relaxed the horse becomes. The same is true of the bell, the ear drum of the hearer, and the hearer himself. Breathing brings the sweet joy of meditation to you. "The sweet joy of meditation" is the great happiness which meditation brings. It is food. If you are nourished by the sweet joy of meditation, you become joyful, fresh, and tolerant, and everyone around you will benefit from your joy.

Although the aim of the fourth method of breathing offered by the Buddha—breathing in and out to make your body calm and at peace—is to bring calmness to the movements of your body, its effect is to bring calmness to your breathing and to your mind also. The calmness of one brings calmness to all three. In the calmness of meditation, discrimination between body and mind does not exist, and you dwell at rest in the state of "body and mind at one," no longer feeling that the subject of meditation exists outside the object of meditation.

The Fourth Subject of Full Awareness:
The Food of the Joy of Meditation (Methods 5-6)

Those who practice meditation should know how to nourish themselves on the joy of meditation, on the peace and joy of meditative concentration, in order to reach real maturity and help the world. Life in this world is both painful and miraculous. The Buddhist traditions of the Southern schools stress the painful side, while the Buddhist traditions of the Northern schools help us realize and appreciate the marvels of life. The violet bamboo, the yellow flowers, the white clouds, and the full moon are all wondrous expressions of the *Dharmakaya*, the body of the Dharma. The body of a human being, although impermanent, without an independent self, and bound to suffering, is also wondrous, infinitely wondrous. The initial joy of meditation is like leaving the city, with its hyperactivity and all its disturbing encounters, going off to the countryside to sit beneath a tree, alone. We feel totally at ease, peaceful and joyful. What a joy, what a relief, like when you complete a difficult examination and feel that you have laid aside all anxiety forevermore.

At the end of a busy day, you can turn off the TV, light a stick of incense to make the room fragrant, sit cross-legged, and begin to practice breathing, with a half-smile. You will feel great joy! This is the initial sensation of the peace and joy of meditation. The fifth breathing method, "I am breathing in and feeling joyful. I am breathing out and feeling joyful," helps us become aware of this sensation. If you can set aside the stresses and complications of your day, you will enter a meditation filled with joy. From this state, it is easy to arrive at the state of peace and happiness.

The sixth method establishes awareness of peace and happiness: "I am breathing in and feeling happy. I am breathing out and feeling happy." This happiness arises when we become free of incessant worrying and preoccupation, and from the fact that the body and mind are at ease.

When we have a toothache, we know that not having a toothache is a pleasurable feeling. But when we do not have a toothache, most of us are unaware of this pleasant feeling. Only after we become blind will we be aware that having eyes to see the blue sky and the white clouds is miraculous. While we can see, we are rarely aware of this miracle. Practicing meditation is to be aware of both what is painful and what is miraculous. Happiness is the nourishment of the meditator, and it is not necessary to look for it outside of ourselves. We only need to be aware of the existence of happiness in order to have it immediately. Pleasant feelings are like the air around us—we can enjoy them as we need them. In Buddhist psychology, it is said there are three kinds of feelings: pleasant, unpleasant, and neutral (neither pleasant nor unpleasant). But when we practice meditation, we know that we can transform neutral feelings into pleasant ones, and nourish ourselves. Pleasant feelings transformed from neutral ones are more healthy and lasting than other pleasant feelings. When we are constantly nourished by the happiness of meditation, we become at ease with ourself and others. We become tolerant and compassionate, and our happiness is transmitted to all those around us. Only if we have peace ourselves can we share peace with others. Only then do we have enough strength and patience to work helping others, facing many hardships with patience and perseverance.

The Fifth Subject of Full Awareness:
Observing Feelings (Methods 7-8)

The seventh and eighth breathing methods aim at the observation of the feelings, all feelings, agreeable and disagreeable. Feelings of irritation, anger, anxiety, weariness, and boredom are disagreeable ones. Whatever feeling is present, the meditation student identifies it, recognizes that it is there, and lights up the sun of his or her awareness in order to illumine it. That is the work of observation. For example, if we are irritated, we must know, "This irritation is in me. I am this irritation," and we breathe in and out in this awareness.

In Buddhist practice, observation meditation is based on non-duality. Therefore, we do not view irritation as an external enemy coming to invade us. We see that we are that very irritation in the present moment. Thanks to this approach, we no longer need to make an effort to oppose, expel, or destroy this irritation. When we practice observation meditation, we do not set up barriers between good and bad in ourselves and transform ourselves into a battlefield. That is the main thing Buddhism seeks to avoid. We must treat irritation with compassion and nonviolence. We can come face to face with our own irritation with a heart filled with love, as if we were face to face with our own baby sister. We can light up the light of awareness which arises from meditative stability, and by breathing in and out mindfully allow the light to shine steadily. Under the light of awareness, irritation is gradually transformed (not destroyed). Every feeling is a field of energy. A pleasant feeling is an energy which can nourish. Irritation is a feeling which can destroy. Under the light of awareness, the energy of irritation can be transformed into an energy which nourishes.

Feelings originate either in the body or in our perceptions. When we suffer from insomnia, we feel fatigue or irritation. This feeling originates in the body. When we misperceive a person or an object, we may feel anger, disappointment, or irritation. This feeling originates in perception. According to Buddhism, our perceptions are often inaccurate and cause us to suffer. The practice of Full Awareness is to look deeply in order to see the true nature of everything and to go beyond our inaccurate perceptions. Seeing a rope as a snake, we will cry out in fear. Fear is a feeling, and mistaking the rope for a snake is an inaccurate perception.

If we live our daily life in moderation, keeping our body in good health, we can diminish painful feelings which originate in the body. By observing each thing clearly and opening the boundaries of our understanding, we can diminish painful feelings originating from perception. To observe a feeling in order to illumine it is to recognize the multitude of causes near and far. To go deeply into what we recognize is to discover the very nature of feeling.

When a feeling of irritation or fear is present, we can be aware of it, nourishing this awareness through breathing. Fully aware of our breathing, with patience, we come to see more deeply into the true nature of this feeling. In seeing, we come to understand. With understanding, there is freedom. The seventh method refers to the activity of the mind: "I am breathing in and am aware of the activities of the mind in me. I am breathing out and am aware of the activities of the mind in me." "Activities" refers to the arising of a feeling, its duration, and its ceasing in order to become something else.

The eighth method aims at the transformation of the energy of feelings: "I am breathing in and making the activities of the mind in me calm and at peace. I am breathing out and making the activities of the mind in me calm and at peace." By observing the true nature of any feeling, we can transform its energy into the energy of peace and joy. When we understand someone, we can accept and love him. Once we have accepted him, there is no longer any feeling of reproach or irritation against him. The energy of the feeling of irritation, in this case, can be transformed into the energy of love.

The Sixth Subject of Full Awareness:
Mastering and Liberating the Mind (Methods 9-12)

The ninth method is the breathing which recognizes the functions of the mind not including the feelings: "I am breathing in and am aware of my mind. I am breathing out and am aware of my mind." Mind (*citta*) is a psychological phenomena, including perception, thinking, reasoning, discriminating, imagining, and all the activities of the subconscious as well. As soon as any psychological phenomenon arises, we should identify it while breathing with awareness. We continue to observe it to shed light on it and see its connection with the whole of our mind.

The first four breathing methods help us become one with our breathing and drop all thinking, discriminating ideas, and imaginings. The ninth method helps us identify psychological phenomena, such as thoughts or imaginings, as they arise. The term *citta* includes all psychological phenomena, such as feelings, perceptions, thoughts, reasoning, and so forth, along with their objects. It does not refer to a single psychological subject, always unchangeable and identical in nature. Mind is a river of psychological phenomena which are always changing, being born and passing away. In this river, the arising, duration, and cessation of any phenomenon is always linked with the arising, duration, and cessation of all other phenomena. To know how to identify psychological phenomena as they arise and develop is an important part of meditation practice. The activities of our mind, often unstable and agitated, are like a torrent of water washing over the rocks. In traditional Buddhist literature, mind is often compared to a monkey which is always swinging from branch to branch or a horse galloping. Once our mind is able to identify what is happening, we will be able to see it clearly and make it calm, and we can feel peace and joy in its stillness. The tenth breathing method is intended to calm the mind: "I am breathing out and making my mind happy and at peace. I am breathing in and making my mind happy and at peace." Compare this with the fourth and eighth methods. The fourth is intended to calm the body, and the eighth is intended to calm the feelings. These three methods can bring us to the land of great bliss, to a state of joy, peace, and relaxation in meditative concentration. This state brings us ease and can nourish the power of our concentration. But we should not stop at this. We can continue by "observing to shed light on it," in order to arrive at an awakened understanding. Only awakened understanding can lead us to complete freedom.

The eleventh method aims at concentrating our mind on a single object. Only when we can concentrate steadily on an object can we observe it. This object can be a physiological phenomenon, such as the breath; a psychological phenomenon, such as a perception or a feeling; or a physical phenomenon, such as a leaf or a stone. All these phenomena are classified as "objects of mind" and they do not exist independently of mind. The object of the concentrated mind is lit up by the light of the mind's observation, like a singer in a spotlight on a stage. The object can be moving in time and space, since it is as alive as the mind which is observing it. In the state of concentration, the subject and object have become one. Breathing is also an object of the concentrated mind. When we put all our attention on the breath, our mind follows that alone, and our mind and breath are one. That is concentration. Concentration is the vector of consciousness pointed at a single object. After practicing with the breath, we can practice with other physiological, psychological, and physical phenomena. Only if there is concentration can the work of observation be achieved.

The twelfth method aims at untying all the knots of the mind: "I am breathing in and liberating my mind. I am breathing out and liberating my mind." Our mind can be tied up by sorrows and memories of the past; or drawn along by anxieties and predictions concerning the future; or held subservient to feelings of irritation, fear, and doubt, in the present; or obscured and confused by inaccurate perceptions. Only by concentrating the mind do we have the capacity to observe and illumine, and be emancipated from obstacles. It is the same as when we try to take knots out of thread. We have to be calm, and we need to take time. By observing our mind in all its subtlety, in a calm and self-contained way, we can free our mind from all confusion.

The Seventh Subject of Full Awareness:
Observing to Shed Light on The True Nature of All Dharmas (Methods 13-16)

The thirteenth method for breathing proposed by the Buddha aims at observation to shed light on the impermanent nature of all dharmas. All phenomena, whether physiological, psychological, or physical, without exception are impermanent. Impermanent does not only mean "here today, gone tomorrow." The meditation on impermanence is a deep, penetrating, and wonderful path of meditation. There is no phenomenon whatsoever with a separate, lasting individuality. All things, without exception, are in endless transformation, and all things are without an independent self. To be impermanent is also to be without-self. This is a fundamental recognition in Buddhism regarding the nature of all that exists.

Impermanence also means Interdependence. The components of the universe depend on one another for their existence. The *Majjhima Nikaya Sutta* says, "This is, because that is. If this is not, then that is not." Impermanence also means Signlessness. The reality of all that exists is beyond every concept and linguistic expression. We cannot go directly to their essential and true nature, because we are accustomed to grasping phenomena through the intermediaries of perception and thought. The categories of perception and thought are "signs." The example of wave and water is often given to help us understand the "signless" nature of all that exists. A wave can be high or low, can arise or disappear, but the essence of the wave—water—is neither high nor low, neither arising nor disappearing. All signs—high, low, arising, disappearing—cannot touch the essence of water. We cry and laugh according to the sign because we have not yet seen the essence. The essence (*svabhava*) is the very nature of everything that is and of the reality of ourselves. Impermanence is also Emptiness. The reality of everything that exists is its signlessness, since it is a reality that cannot be grasped by concepts and words. Because it cannot be grasped, it is called Empty. Emptiness here does not mean nonexistent, as opposed to existent. It means Signless, free from all imprisonment by concepts—birth/death, existent/nonexistent, increasing/decreasing, pure/impure. It says in the *Prajñaparamita Heart Sutra*, "All dharmas are marked with emptiness; they are neither produced nor destroyed, neither defiled nor immaculate, neither increasing nor decreasing." Impermanence also means Aimlessness (*apranihita*). The presence of everything that exists is not to attain a final goal. We cannot add onto the true nature of all that exists, nor can we remove anything from it. It has no origin and no end. We do not need to seek realization outside of all that exists. In the very "stuff" of every dharma, the awakened nature is already fully present.

The fourteenth breathing method aims at observing to shed light on the "fading"[40] nature of all dharmas: "I am breathing in and observing the fading of all dharmas. I am breathing out and observing the fading of all dharmas." All things are without permanence and therefore on the way to dissolution. A rose, a cloud, a human body, an ancient tree, all are on the way to dissolution. Judging from all dharmas right here on the physical plane, all pass through the stages of birth, duration, transformation, and disappearance. The beginning practitioner should observe clearly the impermanent and fading nature of all things, including the Five Aggregates that comprise his or her own self. The Nine Contemplations were the special observation practice with regard to the body used at the time of the Buddha. The Nine Contemplations are the practice of observing to throw light on the decomposition of a corpse from the time when it becomes bloated to the time when it disappears into dust and ashes. The corpse which is the object is any corpse in a cemetery, as well as the corpse of the practitioner. In the *Khoa Hu Luc (Lessons in Emptiness)*, King Trân Thái Tông contemplates as follows:

> Formerly glowing cheeks and pink lips,
> Today cold ashes and white bones.
> Position, renown though unsurpassed,
> They are but part of a long dream.
> However rich and noble you are,
> You are no less impermanent.
> Jealousy, pride, and self-clinging,
> But self is always empty.
> Great strength, ability, and success,
> But in them is no final truth.
> Since the four elements come apart,
> Why discriminate old from young?
> Crevices erode even mountains,
> More quickly the hero is dead.
> Black hair has hardly grown on our head,
> When suddenly it has turned white.

Our well-wisher has just departed,
A mourner arrives on our death.
This six-foot skeleton of dry bones
With what effort it seeks riches.
This wrapping of skin containing blood
Suffers long in its need to love.

This is a way of looking at our body, and it is also a way of looking at our mind. Our mind, which is subtle and quick today, can become slow and senile tomorrow. Rivers, mountains, houses, riches, health—all should be meditated on like this.

Perhaps you will smile and say that this way of contemplation is intended principally to bring us to a pessimistic state of mind, frustrating our love of life and our joy in living. This is both true and not true. Medicine may be bitter, but it will possibly heal our sickness. Reality may be cruel, but to see things as they are will heal us. Reality is the ground of effective liberation. Life passes so quickly, and there is no stopping it from being cut off. The sap of joy flows through every living thing, from the mineral world through the vegetable world, to the world of living beings. Only because we imprison ourselves in the idea of a small self do we create a state of darkness, narrowness, anxiety, and sorrow. According to our narrow view of a truly existing self, life is just my body, my house, my spouse, my children, and my riches. But if we can extend beyond every limit we have created for ourselves, we will see that our life exists in everything, and that the deterioration of phenomena cannot touch that life, just as the arising and disappearing of the waves cannot influence the being of the water. By observing in this way to shed light on the deterioration of everything, we can smile in the face of birth and death and attain a lot of peace and joy in this life.

The fifteenth method helps us free ourselves from individuality, so that we can become part of the whole universe: "I am breathing in and contemplating liberation. I am breathing out and contemplating liberation." Here, liberation is freedom from the concepts of life and death, owning and lacking, increasing and decreasing—all concepts which form the basis of desire and attachment, fear and anxiety, hatred and anger. Liberation here means freedom (*nirvana*), the absence of all boundaries.

The sixteenth method, like the fifteenth, aims at helping us observe in order to shed light on giving up all desire and attachment, fear and anxiety, hatred and anger. Seeing that there is a precious jewel in our pocket, we give up every attitude of craving or coveting like one who is deprived. Seeing that we are lions, we do not long to nurse from a mother deer. Seeing that we are the sun, we give up the candle's habit of fearing the wind will blow us out. Seeing that life has no boundaries, we give up all imprisoning divisions. We see ourselves everywhere, and we see our life everywhere. That is why we go to help all living phenomena, all living species, with the vow of a Bodhisattva, one who has attained great awakening.

Giving up, here, does not mean abandoning something in order to seek something else. It means giving up every comparison, seeing that there is nothing to be removed and nothing to be added, and that the boundary between ourself and the other is not real. The practitioner does not give up the human condition in order to become a Buddha. He or she seeks the Buddha in his or her very own human condition, giving up nothing, and seeking nothing either. That is the meaning of *apranihita*, "aimlessness," also translated as wishlessness. It is the same as Not-Seeking, a concept fully developed in Mahayana Buddhism. Give up in order to be everything, and to be completely free. Many people have already done so, and each one of us can do so also, if we have the intention.

In summary, the order of the Sixteen Breathing Methods is the order of the Four Foundations of Mindfulness: body, feelings, mind, and objects of mind. The intelligent practitioner knows how to regulate and master his or her breath, body, and mind, in order to enhance the power of concentration before proceeding in the work of observation to shed light. Meditation practice is nourishing for body and mind, and can also expand our vision. Expanded vision enables us to go beyond passionate attachment or aversion to life. It makes us joyful, calm, stable, tolerant, and compassionate.

For the practices presented here to have a greater chance of success, the reader is asked to read the *Satipatthana Sutta* and to combine the practice of the teachings of the Buddha in the *Satipatthana* with the practice of the teachings of the *Anapanasati Sutta*.

Notes

[1]Savatthi: the capital of the Kosala kingdom, about 75 miles west of Kapilavastu.

[2]*Bhikkhu*: monk.

[3]The *Pavarana* Ceremony was held at the end of each rainy-season retreat, the annual three-month retreat for Buddhist monks. During the ceremony each monk present invited the assembly to point out the weaknesses he exhibited during the retreat.

The full-moon marked the end of the lunar month. Normally *Pavarana* was held at the end of the month of Assayuja (around October), but during the year in which this sutra was delivered, the Buddha extended the retreat to four months, and the ceremony was held at the end of the month of Kattika (around November).

[4]The full moon day of the retreat's fourth month (*Kattika*) was called *Komudi*, or White Lotus Day, so-named because komuda is a species of white lotus which flowers in late Autumn.

[5]field of merit: Supporting a good community, like planting seeds in fertile soil, is a good investment.

[6]*Arahat* (Sanskrit: *Arhat*): the highest realization according to the early Buddhist traditions. *Arhat* means worthy of respect, deserving. An *Arhat* is one who has rooted out all the causes of affliction and is no longer subject to the cycle of death and birth.

[7]Root of Affliction (Skt: *klesa*, Pali: *klesa*). The ropes which enslave the mind, like greed, anger, ignorance, scorn, suspicion, and wrong views. It is the equivalent to *Asava* (Pali): suffering, pain, the poisons of the mind, the causes which subject us to birth and death, like craving, wrong views, ignorance.

[8]That is, the first 5 of the 10 Ropes of Bondage (Skt. *Samyojana*): (1) caught in the wrong view of self, (2) hesitation, (3) caught in superstitious prohibitions and rituals, (4) craving, (5) hatred and anger, (6) desire for the worlds of form, (7) desire for the formless worlds, (8) pride, (9) agitation, and (10) ignorance. These are the ropes which bind us and hold us enthralled to our worldly situation.

In the Mahayana, the 10 Ropes of Bondage are listed in the following order: desire, hatred, ignorance, pride, hesitation, belief in a real self, extreme views, wrong views, perverted views, views advocating unnecessary prohibitions. The first 5 are called "dull," and the second 5 are called "sharp."

[9]Fruit of Never Returning (*Anagami-phala*): The fruit, or attainment, second only to the fruit of Arahathood. Those who realize the Fruit of Never Returning do not return after this life to the cycle of birth and death.

[10]Fruit of Returning Once More (*Sakadagami-phala*): The fruit, or attainment, just below the Fruit of Never Returning. Those who realize the Fruit of Returning Once More will return to the cycle of birth and death just one more time.

[11]The Fruit of Stream Enterer (*Sotapatti-phala*): the fourth highest fruit, or attainment. Those who attain the Fruit of Stream Enterer are considered to have entered the Stream of Awakened Mind, which always flows into the Ocean of Emancipation.

[12]The Four Foundations of Mindfulness (*Satipatthana*): (1) Awareness of the body in the body, (2) Awareness of feelings in feelings, (3) Awareness of the mind in the mind, (4) Awareness of the objects of the mind in the objects of the mind. For further explication, see Nyanaponika Thera, *The Heart of Buddhist Meditation* (New York: Weiser, 1965) or other translations of the *Satipatthana Sutta*. See also Thich Nhat Hanh, *Being Peace* (Berkeley: Parallax Press, 1987), p. 39.

[13]The Four Right Efforts (Pali: *padhana*): (1) Not to allow any occasion for wrongdoing to arise, (2) Once it has arisen, to find a means to put an end to it, (3) To cause right action to arise when it has not already arisen, (4) To find ways to develop right action and make it lasting once it has arisen.

[14]The Four Bases of Success (*iddhi-pada*): Four roads which lead to realizing a strong mind: diligence, energy, full awareness, and penetration.

[15]The Five Faculties (*indriyana*): Five capacities, or abilities: (1) confidence, (2) energy, (3) meditative stability, (4) meditative concentration, and (5) true understanding.

[16]The Five Powers (*bala*): the same as the Five Faculties, but seen as strengths rather than abilities.

[17]The Seven Factors of Awakening (*bojjhanga*): (1) Full Attention, (2) Investigating Dharmas, (3) Energy, (4) Rapture Beyond the Everyday World (see note 26), (5) Lightness and Peacefulness, (6) Concentration, (7) Equanimity. These are discussed in Section Four of the Sutra.

[18]The Noble Eightfold Path (*atthangika-magga*): the right way of practicing, containing eight elements: (1) Right View, (2) Right Intention, (3) Right Speech, (4) Right Action, (5) Right Livelihood, (6) Right Effort on the path, (7) Right Awareness, (8) Right Meditative Concentration.
   The above practices, from the Four Foundations of Mindfulness, through the Noble Eightfold Path, total 37, and are called *bodhipakkhiya dhamma*, the Components of Awakening.

[19]Lovingkindness, Compassion, Joy, and Equanimity (*brama-vihara*): Four beautiful, precious states of mind, which are not subject to any limitation, often called the Four Limitless Meditations. Lovingkindness is to give joy. Compassion is to remove suffering. Joy is happiness and joy in the joy of others. Equanimity is relinquishing, with no calculation of gain or loss, no clinging to beliefs as the truth, and no anger or sorrow.

[20]Nine Contemplations: the practice of contemplation on the nine stages of disintegration of a corpse, from the time it swells up to the time it becomes dust.

[21]Joy and Happiness: The word *piti* is usually translated "joy," and the word *sukha* is usually translated "happiness." The following example is often used to compare *piti* with *sukha*: Someone travelling in the desert who sees a stream of cool water experiences *piti* (joy), and on drinking the water experiences *sukha* (happiness).

[22]*dharmas*: things, phenomena.

[23]Fading (*viraga*): A fading of the color and taste of each dharma, and its gradual dissolution, and at the same time a fading and gradual dissolution of the color and taste of desire. *Raga* means a color, or dye; here it is also used to mean desire. *Viraga* is thus the fading both of color and of craving.

[24]Liberation, or Emancipation, here means putting an end to the roots of affliction and sorrows by transforming them.

[25]Letting Go, or Relinquishing, here means giving up everything which we see to be illusory and empty of substance.

[26]"Unworldly" or "Rapture Beyond the Everyday World" is the translation of *niramisa*. This is the great joy which is not to be found in the realm of sensual desire.

[27]Discriminating and Comparing: That is to say, discriminating subject from object, comparing what is dear to us with what we dislike, what is gained with what is lost.

[28]Equanimity (Pali: *upekkha*, Skt: *upeksa*): Sometimes translated "indifference." The notion of giving up discriminating and comparing subject/object, like/dislike, gain/loss is fundamental. The Buddhism of the Mahayana school has fully developed this concept.

---

[29]*Sutta* (Sanskrit: *sutra*): a discourse of the Buddha.

[30] 大 安 般 守 意 經

[31]Sutra number 602 in the Revised Chinese Tripitaka.

[32]Sutra number 125 in the Revised Chinese Tripitaka.

[33]Sutra number 606 in the Revised Chinese Tripitaka.

[34]Four Meditative States (Sanskrit: *Rupa Dhyana*, Pali: *Rupa Jhana*)

[35]Four Formless Concentrations (Sanskrit: *Arupa Dhyana*, Pali: *Arupa Jhana*)

[36]See Nyanaponika Thera, *op. cit.* Footnote no. 12.

[37]The method of counting the breath has been widely accepted and has found its way into the sutras and commentaries. The *Ekottaragama* (*Zeng Yi A Han*) (Sutra number 125 in the Revised Chinese Tripitaka, An Ban chapter, books 7 and 8) does not mention the technique of counting the breath, but it does mention the method of combining the breathing with the Four Meditative States. Chapter 23 of the *Xiu Hang Dao Di* (Sutra number 606 in the Revised Chinese Tripitaka, book 5) called "The Breath Counting Chapter," identifies the method of Full Awareness of Breathing with the method of counting the breaths. This sutra also refers to the Four Meditations.

[38]Sutra number 606 in the Revised Chinese Tripitaka, ch. 23.

[39]Sutra number 125 in the Revised Chinese Tripitaka.

[40]See note 23.

About the Author

Thich Nhat Hanh is a Vietnamese Buddhist monk, ordained in the Zen tradition. He is author of *Zen Keys*, *The Sun My Heart*, *Being Peace*, and many other works.

About the Translator

Annabel Laity is a school teacher and Buddhist practitioner, presently living in Plum Village in France.

About Parallax Press

Parallax Press publishes books and tapes on Buddhism and related subjects for contemporary readers. We carry all books by Thich Nhat Hanh in English. For a copy of our free catalogue, please write to:

Parallax Press

P. O. Box 7355

Berkeley, California 94707